Zoom In on Polar Animals

Penguins

Leo Statts

abdopublishing.com

Published by Abdo Zoom™, PO Box 398166, Minneapolis, Minnesota 55439. Copyright © 2017 by Abdo Consulting Group, Inc. International copyrights reserved in all countries. No part of this book may be reproduced in any form without written permission from the publisher. Abdo Zoom™ is a trademark and logo of Abdo Consulting Group, Inc.

Printed in the United States of America, North Mankato, Minnesota
062016
092016

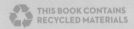
THIS BOOK CONTAINS
RECYCLED MATERIALS

Cover Photo: Shutterstock Images, cover
Interior Photos: iStockphoto, 1, 9, 10–11, 16; Travel Media Productions/Shutterstock Images, 4; Christian Musat/Shutterstock Images, 5; IPGGutenbergUKLtd/iStockphoto, 7; Richard Lindie/iStockphoto, 8; Red Line Editorial, 11, 20 (left), 20 (right), 21 (left), 21 (right); Michal Krakowiak/iStockphoto, 12–13; Ron Smith/Shutterstock Images, 14; Shutterstock Images, 15; Keith Szafranski/iStockphoto, 17; Andre Anita/Shutterstock Images, 18–19

Editor: Emily Temple
Series Designer: Madeline Berger
Art Direction: Dorothy Toth

Publisher's Cataloging-in-Publication Data
Names: Statts, Leo, author.
Title: Penguins / by Leo Statts.
Description: Minneapolis, MN : Abdo Zoom, [2017] | Series: Polar animals |
    Includes bibliographical references and index.
Identifiers: LCCN 2016941136 | ISBN 9781680791884 (lib. bdg.) |
    ISBN 9781680793567 (ebook) | ISBN 9781680794458 (Read-to-me ebook)
Subjects: LCSH: Penguins--Juvenile literature.
Classification: DDC 598.47--dc23
LC record available at http://lccn.loc.gov/2016941136

Table of Contents

Penguins

Penguins are birds.
They cannot fly. But they can
slide on their stomachs.

They can also swim.
They catch food in the water.

Body

Penguins have white stomachs. Their backs are black.

Penguins have **flippers**.

Flippers help them swim fast.

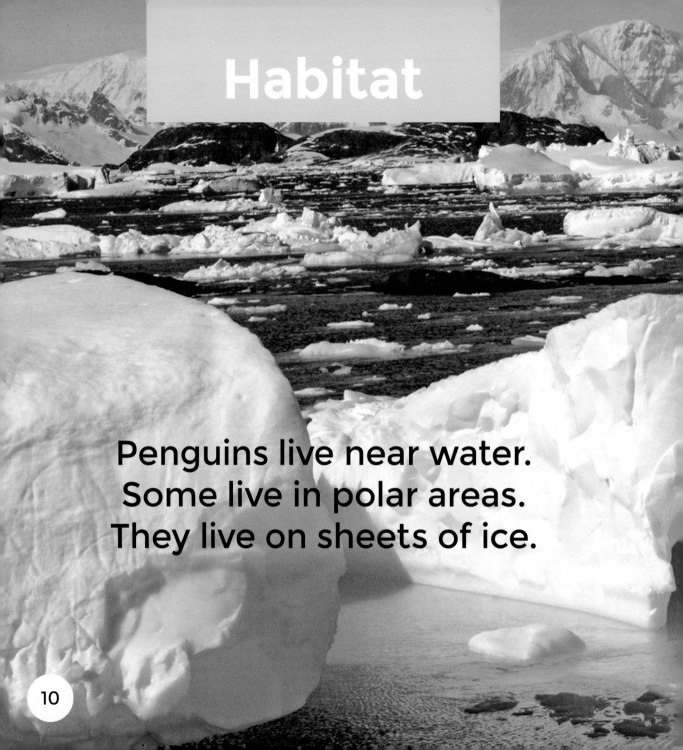

Habitat

Penguins live near water.
Some live in polar areas.
They live on sheets of ice.

Where penguins live

Other penguins
live in warm places.
They live on sandy
beaches. Some live
on small islands.

Food

Penguins hunt for food.
They dive underwater.

14

They eat fish and squid. Sometimes they eat **krill** and other **crustaceans**.

Life Cycle

Penguins lay eggs.
Chicks grow in the eggs.

Then they **hatch**.
They live for
approximately 17 years.

Penguins live in **colonies**. Some have thousands of penguins.

Shortest Height

A little blue penguin is taller than a basketball.

12 in

9.5 in

Tallest Height

An emperor penguin is taller than an acoustic guitar.

3 ft 9 in

3 ft 4 in

Glossary

chick - a baby bird.

colony - a group of animals of one kind living together.

crustacean - any of a group of animals with hard shells that live mostly in water.

flippers - wide, flat limbs sea creatures use for swimming.

hatch - to be born from an egg.

krill - small shrimp-like animals of the open sea.

Booklinks

For more information
on **penguins**, please visit
booklinks.abdopublishing.com

Z**QQ**m™ In on Animals!

Learn even more with the Abdo Zoom
Animals database. Check out
abdozoom.com for more information.

Index